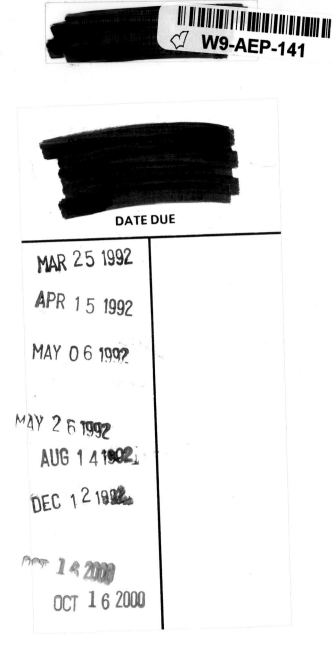

EARLY
AMERICA
1492-1812

Minorities in American History
Volume 1

EARLY AMERICA
1492-1812

by William Loren Katz
illustrated with photographs

Franklin Watts, Inc.
New York / 1974

Frontispiece: the Spanish expeditions that explored America included soldiers, missionaries, and both Europeans and Africans, as well as guides from the native peoples.

For Jacqueline

Cover by Mark Rubin

Photographs courtesy of the author's private collection, with the following exceptions:
Library of Congress — p. 56
New York Public Library Picture Collection —
p. 62 lower left
West Point Museum Collections —
p. 62 lower right

Library of Congress Cataloging in Publication Data

Katz, William Loren.
Early America, 1492-1812.

(His Minorities in American history, v. 1)
SUMMARY: Traces the history of various minority groups in the United States from the arrival of the first settlers to the War of 1812. Includes quotations from contemporary sources.
Bibliography: p.
1. Minorities–United States–Juvenile literature.
2. United States–Race question–Juvenile literature.
[1. Minorities. 2. Race problems] I. Title. II. Series.
E184.A1K3 vol. 1   301.45'1'0420973   73-17283
ISBN 0-531-02676-0

Contents

Minorities in American History

Early America
1492–1812

Slavery to Civil War
1812–1865

Reconstruction and National Growth
1865–1900

From the Progressive Era to the Great Depression
1900–1929

Years of Strife
1929 to 1956

Modern America
1957 to the Present

A British officer tried to convey some picture of the suffering of Africans aboard the slave ships in this painting.

Introduction

From its beginnings, America has been a nation of nations. Its earliest known inhabitants had arrived in the land from Asia many hundreds of years before the Europeans. But the arrival of the newcomers from northern Europe, and the Africans they imported like merchandise and enslaved as laborers, reshaped life on the continents of America.

Basically this was because the Europeans wanted to take or alter what the native Americans had. They sought to drive them from the land and reduce them to bondage while enjoying their hospitality and benefiting from their experience and skill as frontierspeople and farmers. Centuries old native and African cultures were undermined and partially destroyed through the Europeans' religion. European missionaries who accompanied the early explorers had almost as important an impact as the overwhelming arms carried by the explorers.

In the New World the clash of cultures extended beyond race, to religion. Conflict between Christian sects was not uncommon, and hostility toward non-Christians was universal. Catholics, Quakers, and Jews suffered persecution in many of the colonies. In addition, disputes between various nationality groups marked the colonial era in the New World. Wars between England and Spain and France often pitted red, black, and brown men and women against each other.

By the end of this period people from every nation of Europe and Africa had settled in the Americas; all contributed toward its economy and way of life. Some groups had already begun to agitate for their just treatment. Africans organized to protest against slavery. Perhaps foremost among the whites who supported their efforts were the persecuted Quakers. Jews and Catholics had demanded and generally won the right to practice their religion without government repression.

But throughout the colonies the native Americans won few supporters and fewer victories for their way of life. Europeans continued to press them from their land and employ treachery and military methods to achieve their ends.

By the time fifty-five American men met at Philadelphia to write a new Constitution, there was general agreement that government would serve the interests of white men, particularly those of property, without distinction to religion or national origin. Females, nonwhites, and the propertyless were not assured basic protections — for they remained voteless. Because they had chosen to take the native land and to enslave the African, whites had agreed to keep the peace among themselves.

But for all its early hostility toward minorities, the new society provided greater opportunities than any other land for those who were allowed and determined to move up the economic ladder. This may explain why in time the bigotry among white ethnic and religious groups was able to diminish to so great an extent. A further explanation may be that unity among whites was necessary to retain control of the rights and property seized from nonwhites.

It Began
with
Columbus

For all, except the original inhabitants, America began with Columbus. For all, including the native Americans, bigotry in the New World began with Columbus. A fearless and determined mariner, he sailed from a Spain steeped in religious and racial bitterness. Along with their courage and daring, Columbus and his crew carried this animosity on their historic voyage. In fact, the expedition to the Americas followed two violent acts against minorities in Spain.

In 1492 King Ferdinand and Queen Isabella felt free to devote themselves to the pursuit of overseas expansion. They had just solved two minority "problems." That January they had expelled the Moors, who six centuries earlier had come from Africa to Spain. Because they were dark-skinned and Muslim rather than Catholic, they were considered dangerous and, despite their six hundred years in Spain, were driven from the continent.

On the August day when the *Niña*, *Pinta*, and *Santa Maria* weighed anchor at Palos for their great voyage, Spanish Jews in Cádiz were waiting for ships to take them from their homeland. The monarchy and papacy had ordered Spain to expel its Jews as dangerous heretics. Some had converted to Christianity to escape persecution, but it was no use. They were considered even more dangerous than those who asserted their Judaic traditions. "The whole accursed race of Jews, male and female, of twenty years and upwards," declared a Spanish official, "might be purified by fire."

The glowing fires of this kind of hatred helped launch Columbus's expedition. Monies seized from Jews helped pay for it. The day he sailed from Palos, Columbus praised his king and queen for their handling of the Jews.

When he landed in the West Indies, Columbus continued to act in keeping with the tradition he had left. To gain information from the people to whom he gave the name "Indians" he later reported to the king, "I took some of the natives by force." Whether force was necessary at that moment will never be known. But soon after his arrival he wrote to King Ferdinand and Queen Isabella: "So tractable, so peaceable are these people that I swear to your Majesties there is not in the world a better nation." The reward for possessing such outstanding characteristics was strange indeed. For Columbus concluded he had found a people ripe for slavery, exploitation, or death. He chained ten Arawaks and sent them across the sea as a present to the Spanish king.

Columbus came to a basic conclusion about the native population. They should be "made to work . . . and adopt our ways." He set this task in motion by shipping hundreds of men and women to the slave markets of Spain. Although two hundred died on the first voyage and their bodies were thrown into the sea, the trade in human beings across the Atlantic continued. "From here, in the name of the Blessed Trinity," Columbus wrote to his king and queen, "we can send all the slaves that can be sold."

The Cherokees View Columbus Day

In 1972, as most Americans prepared to celebrate Columbus Day, a Cherokee newspaper in North Carolina denounced the idea. In urging that the holiday be abolished, they called it a "racist insult." It honored "a trader in Indian slaves," they pointed out. But few who celebrated Columbus Day knew what the Cherokees were talking about.

COLUMBUS AND THE "INDIANS"

Thinking he had landed near the coast of India, his original destination, Columbus called the inhabitants he met "Indians." He died not realizing he had found a continent that Europeans had never reached before. But his error lived on, even after Europeans knew the land was not India. The one million natives, grouped in six hundred different societies — as distinguishable from each other as European cultural groups — were still called "Indians."

Columbus also established the basic Spanish land policy in the Americas. Called the *encomienda* system, it granted native land to Spaniards and gave them the right to enslave enough people to work the soil. The new landowners determined such matters as pay and working conditions.

Many of the *conquistadors* who followed Columbus brought their own brand of Christianity and civilization to the Americas. Vasco Balboa, crossing Panama to the Pacific in 1513, destroyed a village whose inhabitants tried to halt his progress. After the surrender, his men killed six hundred prisoners with swords and unleashed savage dogs on women, children, and the elderly. In Mexico, Hernando Cortez tried to destroy the civilization he found there. Precious documents were tossed on bonfires, public officials burned at the stake, and ordinary citizens enslaved. Convinced of Spanish invincibility, the Aztec leader Montezuma called on his people to give the conquistadors what they wanted. Instead, they stoned Montezuma to death and drove the Spaniards from their capital.

But the European onslaught continued. In Peru, the four Pizarro brothers discovered a rich Inca culture, but all they wanted from it was its monetary wealth. The Pizarros captured the Inca ruler Atahualpa and held him for ransom. But even though his subjects provided the fortune in gold and silver that was demanded, Atahualpa was murdered. Soon the brothers fell to fighting among themselves over their new wealth.

Spanish soldiers smash their way into Mexico City led by Cortez.

Left: Europeans found complex cultures among the many peoples of the Americas. A European artist sketched this Mexican marriage ceremony.

Defender of
Humanity

The first great campaign to convince Europeans to treat minorities
humanely was launched by just one man — Bartolomé de las Casas,
who, with his father, sailed to the Americas on Columbus's third
voyage in 1498, seeking wealth and adventure. Father and son settled
down on a West Indies plantation worked by native slave labor. But
Bartolomé was troubled by the injustice before him and joined the
Dominican Brotherhood. In 1510 he became a priest, the first ordained
in the New World.

By then Spain had discovered that undermining native religions
and replacing them with Christianity helped to pacify local popula-
tions. Priests accompanied the conquistadors, seeking to baptize away
resistance. Las Casas was selected to aid the conquistadors in Cuba. He
saw villages burned, native leaders tortured or slain, and local inhabitants crushed by fear, violence, and death.

The slaughter of native societies moved Las Casas to action. On
more than one occasion he returned to Spain to report the massacre of
natives by the greedy conquistadors. He protested not only mass
murder, but also slavery and the use of religion to hide the Spanish
crimes. His campaign began to bear fruit. The king proclaimed Las
Casas "Protector of the Indians" and sent him back to the Americas

*Bartolomé Las Casas devoted his life to ending the
European extermination of America's native population.*

[8]

to chart reforms. When Las Casas found himself consistently undermined by those Spaniards seeking profit from native labor, he returned to the Spanish court to demand greater powers.

During his lifetime Las Casas also catalogued and denounced the crimes of the Christians in a number of books. He cited statistics of mass murders and argued eloquently about the results of the drive for gold: "The reason why the Christians have killed and destroyed such infinite numbers of souls, is solely because they have made gold their ultimate aim, seeking to load themselves with riches in the shortest possible time." He depicted the enormity of the carnage: "Tyranny

RACE AND SLAVERY
IN THE AMERICAS

For all its brutality and evil, the bondage that developed in the Catholic countries of South America inflicted less damage upon its victims that that which grew in the American southern colonies. A powerful Catholic church, interested in the soul of black and red people, offered some protection for slaves. In the English colonies no church or power dared to tell a slaveholder how to deal with his property. Slaveholders in America dictated to government and clergy.

Since Catholic priests believed in the redemption of the slave, they viewed him merely as a man who became a slave by circumstances. Racism in the English colonies, however, emphasized that the red and black man were inferior and therefore entitled to neither land, labor, nor life without white consent. Not viewing slaves as members of an "inferior race," the Catholic colonies allowed slaves to liberate themselves, bring suit in court for abuses by masters, and keep families together.

Martin De Porres, an African born in Lima, Peru, at the end of the sixteenth century, became the world's first black priest. Almost three centuries would pass before a black man in the United States could become a priest.

Early in the seventeenth century, runaway slaves in the Portuguese colony of Brazil fled to the woods and organized their own settlement. They called themselves the Republic of Palmares, and for protection built three huge walls and stocked arms and ammunition. Twenty thousand liberated men and women lived in Palmares. One leader, Zambi, was described by the Portuguese as "a Negro of singular courage, great presence of mind, and unusual devotion."

Within its walls, free men and women retained African customs and established tribunals of justice. Twenty-five times soldiers tried to storm its walls only to be driven back. It was so well defended, noted one Portuguese, "as to be lacking only in artillery."

Finally, it was overwhelmed. One legend tells how the men of Palmares leaped over a cliff rather than face capture. It was no legend that this free city of African men, women, and children lasted for sixty-nine years.

---

wrought by their devastations, massacres and slaughters are so monstrous, that the blind may see it, the deaf hear it, and the dumb recount it." He foresaw the wrath of a just God who "will punish Spain and all her people with inevitable severity."

Las Casas helped eliminate a number of the worst abuses of the Spanish conquest. The massacres were halted, slavery was ended, the encomienda land system was changed, and supervision of native societies was placed under priests. In Guatemala, Peru, and elsewhere on the South American continent, he exposed inhuman conditions, battled unjust landlords, and converted tribes to his brand of Christianity. However, his effort to establish a model community run jointly by Europeans and native Americans failed after a year. An attack by Europeans on a neighboring village, which drew the natives from Las Casas's community off to help their brothers defend themselves, was at least partly to blame.

In addition to launching reforms in the Americas, Las Casas devoted himself to the battle for people's minds. One historian commissioned by King Charles V was claiming that atrocities against natives were necessary to control them. It was not unusual for such scholars to replace a blood-soaked heritage with legends of white knights and Christian saints carrying European civilization to hopeless barbarians. Las Casas countered by writing his own *History of the Indies*. His stark, powerful story, which totaled about nine hundred pages, was suppressed for centuries and not published until 1909.

Spaniards learned about the new overseas possessions not from Las Casas but from Gonzalo Fernández de Oviedo y Valdés, official historian of the conquest. According to his written accounts, the original Americans were "naturally lazy and vicious, melancholic, cowardly, and in general a lying, shiftless people." To justify Spanish exploitation, Oviedo created stereotypes of their behavior.

Their chief desire is to eat, drink, worship heathen idols, and commit bestial obscenities. What could one expect from a people whose skulls are so thick and hard that the Spanish had to take care in fighting not to strike on the head lest their swords be blunted.

Toward the end of his long life Las Casas had made a last effort to prevent the slaughter of the native population of the New World. He proposed that each Spaniard with land be permitted to import twelve Africans as laborers. His aims were conversions to Christianity and a paternalistic, small-scale, agricultural system relying on African labor. What followed was a brutal, dehumanizing perpetual bondage that replaced native men, women, and children with those from Africa.

Viewing the beginning of this nightmare, Las Casas renounced his own suggestion and rejected the enslavement of any people. But his cries were to no avail. At that point no voice could have halted those bent on deriving profits from slave-trading and slave labor.

[12]

The African
Slave Trade

The African slave trade began slowly. A half-century before Columbus landed, Portuguese seamen who reached Africa's west coast brought Prince Henry the Navigator a present of ten Africans. Portugal soon led in this brisk trade, and in 1493 the pope awarded its merchants a monopoly since they promised to baptize their human commerce in transit to the New World.

This lucrative trade soon attracted nobles and pirates from every nation in Europe. Its impact upon black and white was depicted by Thomas Branagan, an Irish seaman aboard a slave ship in the eighteenth century. In Africa Branagan witnessed the boarding:

> *Children are torn from their distracted parents; parents from their screaming children; wives from their frantic husbands; husbands from their violated wives; brothers from their loving sisters; sisters from their affectionate brothers. See them collected in flocks, and like a herd of swine, driven to the ships. They cry, they struggle, they resist; but all in vain. No eye pities; no hand helps.*

The four-month trip to the Americas was a nightmare of terror for the more than fifteen million Africans who survived. Packed below decks "spoon fashion," with scarcely room to move, Africans found the stench and heat intolerable. Olaudah Equiano, kidnapped at the age of eleven from Benin, described a typical voyage from Africa.

"The shrieks of the women, and the groans of the dying, rendered the whole a scene of horror almost inconceivable." Africans taken on deck for exercise often leaped overboard as soon as they were unshackled. Some below decks tried to swallow their tongues and others tried to starve themselves to death, such as in the scene of a slave ship at left. The man at the far right had tried to starve himself to death to escape a life of slavery. Instead, he is being forced to eat by two members of the crew.

RESISTANCE ABOARD
THE SLAVE SHIPS

Every precaution was taken to prevent Africans from speaking aboard slave ships. People from many tribes were mixed together so they could not communicate easily. Given less than necessary food and water kept slaves weak and frightened. Men and women who acted courageously were punished or killed.

Crewmen searched the slave quarters each day, according to a seaman, "to see whether they have . . . any pieces of iron, or wood or knives." Still the Africans mutinied, using their chains as weapons. One hundred times they seized control of ships, killed the crews or set them adrift, and tried to find their way back to Africa. Captain Philip Drake, a captain for fifty years, reported: "The Negroes fought like wild beasts. . . . Slavery is a dangerous business at sea as well as ashore."

Conquest
of the
Southwest

The first foreigner to enter Arizona and New Mexico was unlike other conquistadors in many ways. Esteban, Stephen Dorantes, or Little Stephen, as he was variously called, was an African and a slave. As the advance scout for a 1539 expedition searching for Cibola, the fabled native Seven Cities of Gold, he proved himself able to learn native languages quickly and to breach cultural barriers. Heading northwest, carrying a decorated gourd as a symbol of peace and friendship, he attracted three hundred native men and women to his march. Then, under circumstances never completely known, he disappeared.

However, tales of his success in reaching Arizona and New Mexico, and embroidered stories of golden cities, soon led to explorations by Hernando de Soto, Francisco Coronado, and Juan Cabrillo. These men opened the southwestern United States, whose door Esteban had left ajar, to European penetration.

Unlike Esteban, de Soto, Coronado, and Cabrillo became textbook heroes, known to millions of school children. Historians have either ignored Esteban or treated him shabbily. They usually have cast him

The four survivors of the Narvaez expedition of 1528 included three Spaniards and Esteban, an African (far right). They survived for almost a decade by trading with Indians and acting as "medicine men."

[16]

as a clown who hoodwinked native men and molested their women. While the same claims have been made against white explorers, these are not the exploits for which they are remembered. But traditional beliefs held by whites about black character and achievement often have led to negative accounts of black figures in American history.

De Soto and Coronado followed Esteban's footsteps, but their approach to native societies followed the tradition denounced by Las Casas. From the Carolinas to Oklahoma, de Soto murdered men, women, and children, except for youths he could sell as slaves or leaders he could hold for ransom. Coronado unleashed a similar carnage from Kansas to Arizona.

Birth of
La Raza

Those who are now called "American Indians" were not alone in the Southwest. The people who would later call themselves Mexican-American, Chicano, Indo-Hispanic, or La Raza lived in the New World before the birth of Christ. Some lived in the stone apartments of the Zuni society of New Mexico, and others in the bustling cities of the Aztec Empire in Mexico. The Aztecs were accomplished engineers, skilled in metal work, music, weaving, and picture writing. Their scientists developed a calendar, and their literary figures recorded their history and their progress. The entire Aztec culture was based on a complex system of government and universal education of the young. Even conquered regions were allowed a measure of independence.

The arrival of an alien culture from overseas immediately challenged the old ways. When the conflict was not military it was cultural and centered on differences in religious beliefs and practices. Spaniards were determined to convert Aztecs, Zunis, Pueblos, and all other societies to Christianity. Natives knew this was part of an overall plan to subdue them by substituting a white God and culture for their own. The king of Spain realized that at the approach of his missionaries, the natives "flee for the purpose of preventing interference with their manner and custom of life."

The struggle between Christianity and native American culture continued for centuries. Viewing native opposition to missionaries as akin to murder and robbery, the Spanish crown ordered soldiers to

In California a Christian missionary seeks to convert the natives to the European religion.

crush the opposition his priests could not handle. Villages were burned, native priests murdered, and stunned "pagans" were forced to convert to an alien religion.

Before the end of the seventeenth century, the Pueblo society mounted a major revolt against Spanish military and religious control. After five years of planning, Pueblo religious and lay leaders drove two thousand Spaniards back to Mexico City and killed four hundred. Priests were slain, churches set aflame, and religious objects buried in manure. In a final act of defiance Pueblos renounced their Christian marriages. Many plunged into rivers and, with potions supplied by their own religious leaders, "washed away" their baptismal names and the holy oils of the Catholics.

This insurrection also aimed at regaining possession of land and restoring their ancient customs. Popé, chief of the rebellion, commanded his followers to divide the huge Spanish estates and run them cooperatively. This insurrection lasted thirteen years. It was the most successful resistance to foreigners mounted in the New World. But it ended, and Spanish troops and arms restored foreign domination over the region.

Out of the conflict and deaths, a new people began to emerge that blended the cultural contributions of native and Spanish civilizations. Enemy soldiers married women in occupied towns, and children were born who hated neither native nor Spaniard. A Catholic church, accepted in time by all, blessed marriages across racial lines. La Raza had been born in the New World.

Jamestown

Great myths have grown up around the original Americans and the earliest Europeans. The former, we have been told, were ignorant savages, and the latter all came seeking religious and political liberty. Actually, Europeans came seeking wealth and better economic opportunities. Many were sent by investment firms such as the London Company. At once they challenged the native way of life, religion, and philosophy, and they could not understand the native view of property.

The original Americans embraced a theology that saw nature as a mother to all creatures, human and animal. Land existed for the use of each, never as the exclusive property of anyone. Individuals were esteemed for their qualities and skills, not their titles, wealth, or power. Particular care was given to the elderly and the young. The former carried forth the tribal traditions, teaching the latter.

Fifty years before the settlements at Jamestown and Plymouth, five native societies formed an alliance and government. The Mohawk, Seneca, Oneida, Cayuga, and Onandaga united in the Iroquois Confederacy to prevent warfare. Later they accepted the Tuscarora. For two centuries this combination ruled peacefully from the Great Lakes to Pennsylvania. Women played a prominent part in their deliberations.

To promote harmony, the confederation relied on each individual member and on cooperation among all the societies. Its forty-nine chiefs were chosen by mothers, who were selected by each tribe. Through its chiefs each society had votes in the Iroquois Council.

When there was disagreement, the chairman would keep the discussion going until paths to agreement could be found. Social disapproval or angry words was usually sufficient punishment to discipline members.

Europeans emerged from a very different type of society. Their continent was dominated by kings or rich nobles whose aim was to increase their wealth. Their only opposition came from rich merchants who wanted to run the government so they could make greater profits. Rich and poor alike, therefore, developed a hunger for land and money. People, land, business were all viewed as means of making profits rather than of helping people. Religion, culture, and learning were all bent toward this end.

In schools, churches, markets, legislative halls, and books, the European thirst for profit and land was placed first. Teacher, minister, and noble spoke for it and endowed it with morality and goodness.

In Jamestown, Virginia, the first permanent English colony, the worlds of Europe and America met and clashed. Schoolbooks tell of newcomer and native working together and finally joining in the first Thanksgiving. Like most legends, this provides only a portion of the truth.

The generosity of the natives and the iron will of Captain John Smith saved the colony from disaster. The Powhatan Confederacy of Algonquin nations provided the English with corn and bread. This generosity was repaid by English efforts to steal more from the natives. Finally, in 1609 Chief Powhatan confronted Captain John Smith over European greed. He asked three pointed questions:

Why will you take by force what you may obtain by love? Why will you destroy us who supply you with food? What can you get by war?

English settlers continued to steal from the Algonquins.

The newcomers bickered among themselves as well. Mild anger grew to bitter discord. Those willing to work for survival were pitted against those who felt labor was below their station in life. Iron pistol in hand, a determined John Smith informed all that those who did not

[23]

work would not eat. He was often all that stood between the men and starvation, but he was resented for his dictatorial rule. The colonists successfully demanded that he be recalled to England and replaced by another governor.

With Smith's departure, a "starving time" descended on the colony.

In eight months, the population of Jamestown fell from five hundred to sixty. When put to a vote, only one colonist wished to remain in the New World. A new governor arrived to replace idleness and discontent with rigid work and church schedules. Dour men were ordered to pick up tools again, and to attend church, once on Thursdays and twice on Sundays. At ten each morning and four each afternoon all were required to halt their labors for prayers. The new governor never considered the personal or religious choices of the colonists.

In addition to fighting among themselves, from the beginning colonists antagonized friendly Algonquins. Most infuriating was the English habit of stealing food and tools. To cement friendship one British governor offered to marry Pocahontas's sister. But intermarriage with natives, acceptable in Spanish colonies, was frowned upon by the British. A more typical English answer was offered by another Jamestown governor. During one of Pocahontas's frequent visits to the town, she was seized for ransom. Whenever her countrymen appeared ready to meet the price, the governor raised it. A relationship that rested firmly on threat and deception was bound to explode.

Into this unsettled racial mixture, another element was added in 1619. A Dutch ship sailed into Jamestown and traded twenty Africans for food and water. They were quickly sent to work on the expanding tobacco plantations. Originally they were considered indentured servants, whose liberty was granted after a period of faithful service, usually seven years. But as the first Africans who would labor without pay in the United States, they were the first to begin a racial slavery that would not end for two and a half centuries. By 1660 the legal status of black indentured servants had changed to perpetual bondage. In the future all children born to black slave mothers were to be slaves forever.

The Virginia House of Burgesses, America's first legislative body, met in 1619, that summer when the first Africans arrived, to consider laws for the colony. Some twenty-two burgesses had been elected from eleven districts. No sooner had the twenty-two men convened than they faced angry workmen demanding representation. Lowicki, Stefanski, Mata, Zarencia, Bogdan, and Sadowski were highly respected in the colony for their craft in making pitch and tar. However, not being Anglo-Saxons, but Poles, they had been denied the right to vote for burgesses. They downed their tools, marched to the House of Burgesses, and halted proceedings until their rights were established.

The records of the London Company show that "some dispute" then took place, and the Polish workmen were granted the franchise and "made free as any inhabitant there." Black and red men in Jamestown found no such easy hurdle. They faced an insurmountable wall.

In 1622 conflict with the Algonquins exploded, and Jamestown was besieged. When the smoke had cleared most of its inhabitants lay dead. Edward Waterhouse, a leader of the London Company in Jamestown, proclaimed a vengeful new policy. It mixed lust for property with claims of native inferiority. Waterhouse proposed a final solution to the "problem" of native neighbors of the English colony.

Our hands which before were tied with gentleness and fair usage, are now set at liberty by the treacherous violence of the savages. [Now we may] by right of war and the law of nations, invade the country and destroy them who sought to destroy us, whereby we shall enjoy their cultivated places.

Waterhouse urged his countrymen to strike "by force, by surprise, by famine in burning their corn." In less than a generation, the Algonquins near Jamestown were almost wiped out.

The Plymouth Colony

Five years before the *Mayflower* landed its Pilgrim settlers, a British sea captain paused at what is now Plymouth, Massachusetts. By the time he left, he had infected some natives with smallpox and taken others as slaves. Upon the Pilgrims' arrival and discovery of this news, one rejoiced in this "Wonderful Preparation" by "the Lord Jesus Christ" that virtually destroyed the tribe "chiefly young men and children, the very seeds of increase."

The government that the Pilgrims established extended to the natives within reach. Although it operated on land seized from natives, it nevertheless treated them as trespassers. Pilgrim laws against blasphemy were also enforced upon natives, who had no interest in this new concept.

Captain Miles Standish, military director of the colony and folk hero to generations of schoolchildren, preferred to deal with native societies through sudden death rather than through diplomacy. To settle one dispute, he lured four unarmed natives into a room, bolted the door, and hacked them to pieces. After killing a few more, he made sure a survivor carried the tale of his fiendishness back to the tribe.

European hostility, even in these early years, quickly moved toward genocide as the basic approach to relations with local tribes. One night in 1637 the Massachusetts militia staged a surprise attack on a Pequot village. Governor William Bradford depicted the massacre from the viewpoint of a civilized Christian in mortal combat with inferiors:

It was a fearful sight to see them frying in the fire and the streams of blood quenching the same and horrible was the stink and stench thereof. But the victory seemed a sweet sacrifice and they [the soldiers] gave praise thereof to God.

Reverend Increase Mather, spiritual guide of the Puritans, called upon his congregation to give thanks to God "that on this day we have sent six hundred heathen souls to hell."

The Pilgrims had been allowed to settle on land owned by the Wampanoags through the courtesy of their leader, Massassoit. Because a colonist once restored him to health, Massassoit repeatedly ignored the angry charges of his followers that Europeans were dividing the tribes and undermining the chiefs through Christian conversions. With Puritan aid Massassoit became wealthy and powerful, and more easily able to quiet his restless warriors. He even asked the Plymouth court to give English names to his two sons. Wamsutta and Metacomet became Alexander and Philip.

THE PEOPLE WHO SOLD MANHATTAN

When Henry Hudson sailed his *Half Moon* up the river that now bears his name, he found "the natives were good people." However, this did not prevent the Dutch settlers from pursuing a hostile and destructive policy toward them. In 1642 the Dutch governor had his soldiers destroy a native village of 120 men, women, and children. According to Chief Flying Hawk, all were "asleep in their wigwams." As flames engulfed the village, people were bayoneted, babies thrown into the river, and limbs severed. David De Vries, a Dutch leader who was present, found the brutality enough to "move a heart of stone."

The slaughtered tribe had originally greeted the Dutch upon their arrival in the New World by offering them hospitality and provisions. In 1626 this tribe sold Manhattan Island to the Dutch for twenty-four dollars in trinkets.

In 1662 the old chief died, and Wamsutta became king. British officials summoned him for a conference and dispatched soldiers to fetch him when he did not appear. After a long trip, the young king was questioned for hours on his loyalty to the British. By the time the British excused him, Wamsutta was dying of fever.

At the age of twenty-four, Metacomet became chief and sought revenge and began making preparations for war. In 1675 he launched his 20,000 warriors on 52 towns, destroying 12, and killing nearly 1,000 colonists. Besides facing 50,000 English and superior weapons, he also had to contend with traitors purchased by the enemy. His chief allies were killed or betrayed, and his wife and son were kidnapped and sold as slaves in the West Indies. He told his countrymen that the foe had smashed treaties, disregarded native customs, and murdered men, women, and children, whose "spirits cry to us for revenge."

But before he could drive the Europeans from his land, King Philip, as the Europeans called him, was captured and murdered by a traitor. His severed head was sent to Plymouth where it was placed high on a pole in the main street. For twenty-five years it remained a grisly reminder of white power. It also symbolized the change in race relations from the era of Massassoit to his son Metacomet.

Native Gifts

There is no doubt that the survival of the Europeans depended upon the generosity and skills of the native inhabitants of the New World. No settlement would have lasted without the contributions of the neighboring tribes. Yet, this came about as the native population was being decimated by European diseases, swords, methods of warfare, and insatiable greed. Those who dealt honorably or fairly with their neighboring tribes are very few — leaders such as William Penn and Roger Williams, who themselves were persecuted by other Europeans for their religious beliefs.

From native Americans the newcomers learned how to clear forests and prepare the land for crops. Fishheads could be used as fertilizer, traps constructed to provide game, and birch bark canoes built for travel and fishing. From animals came food and the skins for clothing and shelter. Twenty major agricultural products and forty minor ones were introduced to Europeans by American natives. The first Thanksgiving in Plymouth consisted of food grown and contributed to those who gave thanksgiving to their Christian God from those considered uncivilized and pagan.

Had they been of a mind to, the settlers from abroad might have learned even more from the native societies. An intense desire to merge one's life with the environment rather than destroy either environment or life dominated these societies. Economic, political, and

*European attacks on native tribes were frequent,
sudden, merciless and often without provocation.*

educational activities were marked by cooperation. There were, of course, also conflicts between tribes, some of which at times became violent and prolonged. Religion was an intimate part of all life, not merely a separate portion to be observed on a designated day or hour. Along with the potatoes, squash, corn, pumpkins, maple sugar, melons, and cucumbers, the white settlers had the opportunity to use other less tangible gifts of the neighboring native societies. But for the most part they did not.

THE FOODS AND
DEVICES OF AMERICANS

The Europeans claimed they "discovered" a "New World." But their very survival depended upon people who had lived there for centuries.

The contribution of these native societies has been enormous. Almost half of the world's crops were first grown by native Americans and known to whites after Columbus landed. In addition to the staples of potatoes and corn, there was sweet potato, manioc, squash, tomatoes, pumpkins, pineapples, beans, and a wide variety of other fruit and vegetables. The world's cotton is derived from an American species.

Devices invented by native Americans include canoes, snowshoes, moccasins, dog sleds, hammocks, and smoking pipes. They gave the world the rubber ball, central to athletic contests of today. Native designs have influenced crafts, jewelry, and manufactured goods.

The movement to save the environment has returned to ideas about life first formulated by native Americans. The fields of medicine and child psychology are increasingly examining the experience and expertise of the first Americans. The freedom and self-discipline of native Americans inspired philosophers of the democratic revolution all over the world.

Black Hawk, leader of the Sauk-Fox nation, said:

We can only judge what is proper and right by our standard of right and wrong, which differs widely from the whites . . . . The whites may do bad all their lives, and then, if they are sorry for it when about to die, all is well! But with us it is different: we must continue throughout our lives to do what we conceive to be good. If we have corn and meat, and know of a family that have none, we divide with them. If we have more blankets than sufficient, and others have not enough, we must give to them that want.

This is not to say that all native Americans were virtuous and peace-loving. There were evil natives and warlike tribes, and some native practices, such as human sacrifice or torture, were viewed by the Europeans as "savage." But America was a relatively peaceful land before the arrival of the newcomers from across the ocean.

Religion and the Battle for People's Minds

From the time of their arrival in the New World, Europeans groped for arguments to justify their greed. In 1609 British poet Robert Gray announced the world's land was largely held by "unreasonable creatures, or by brutish savages." Their "godless ignorance" entitled them to none of it, he concluded. His countrymen in Jamestown and Plymouth would quickly put this concept into practice.

Reverend Cotton Mather, a Puritan minister, soon added a religious note to the argument. "Though we know not when or how these Indians first became inhabitants of this mighty continent," he explained, "yet we may guess that probably the devil decoyed these miserable savages hither in hopes that the gospel of the Lord Jesus Christ would never come here to destroy or disturb his absolute power."

Native societies repeatedly resisted missionary efforts to convert them to Christianity. They suspected that the white man's religion was merely another way to impose his will on them. Some tried to battle Christianity with logic. Chief Susquehanna was unmoved by the arguments advanced by a Swedish missionary to his Conestogas. Instead he asked the missionary a few questions. Are Conestogas "more virtuous . . . or more vicious" than Christians? If Christians needed less help from God, then why was the Bible in English? If they needed more aid, why did they come out to aid the Conestogas instead of aiding their own people first? Stymied, the missionary forwarded these perplexing questions to his superiors.

A hunchback, four feet seven inches in height, with a large head and flowing beard, Benjamin Lay frightened more people with his ideas than with his looks. An emigrant from England, he settled in Barbados and remained there for thirteen years, until he was fifty-four. Espousing his Quaker religion and associating with natives and Africans, he easily stirred anger and fear.

In 1731 he migrated to America and six years later wrote a book, *All Slave-Keepers that Keep the Innocent in Bondage, Apostates.* Benjamin Franklin published it. The Philadelphia Quakers denounced Lay and his book, and expelled him. However, for the rest of his life he considered himself a Quaker. He turned his efforts to reforming all Quakers on the slavery issue. Once he stood barefoot before a Quaker meeting hall in the snow. To those who expressed concern for his welfare, he answered they ought instead to show concern for slaves — their condition was far worse.

One time he kidnapped the child of a slaveholding family. After the parents became frantic, he returned the child. If they worried about their child, he lectured them, can they imagine how slave parents feel? Slave children can be sold anytime the master wishes.

Twenty years after the Quakers expelled him for his anti-slavery views, their Yearly Meeting expelled all slaveholders. "Thanksgiving and praise be rendered unto the Lord God," Lay rejoiced, "I can now die in peace." He died the next year. Never popular, he was more interested in ending evil than making friends.

Most astounding to various tribes was the gulf between Christian word and deed. In 1792, after most Delawares had been converted by missionaries, their village was pillaged by settlers. Converted and unconverted were massacred. The village chief lamented the many deaths and the hyprocrisy of Christians: "While they held the big Book in one hand, in the other they held murderous weapons . . . .

They killed those who believed in their Book as well as those who did not. They made no distinctions."

Another time two missionaries to the Delawares were rebuffed because whites held blacks in slavery. If blacks were enslaved because of their color, the Delawares wondered "why a red color should not equally justify the same treatment." The missionaries reported that "when they saw the black people among us restored to freedom and happiness" the Delawares would be willing to listen to Christian spokesmen. After all, concluded the Delawares, "a people who had suffered so much and so long" at white hands were entitled to first attention by Christians.

Puritans viewed the appearance of slave ships in religious terms. Although Reverend Mather denounced the trade in Africans as "a spectacle that shocks humanity," he felt God had put these Africans "in your hands. Who can tell what good He has brought them for?" The blacks would remain to labor and become Christians.

ANTHONY BENEZET, HUGUENOT, QUAKER, AND ANTISLAVERY VOICE

No man in his day did more to rid his adopted nation of bondage than did Anthony Benezet, born to a Huguenot family in France in 1713. At age sixteen he joined the Society of Friends and at eighteen he journeyed to America. Before the American Revolution he published three major antislavery volumes. His labors prodded Europeans Thomas Clarkson and John Wesley to work against slavery.

Before he died in 1784, Benezet published a work assailing the mistreatment of native Americans and telling of their achievements. He was among the first to dispute the assumption of white natural superiority. "That the blacks are inferior in their capacities," he wrote, "is a vulgar prejudice, founded on . . . pride or ignorance." He devoted much of his life to educating nonwhites to prove they have "as great a variety of talents as amongst a like number of whites."

In 1818 a Spanish official, Don Luis de Onís, wrote the United States Secretary of State a simple justification for African slavery in the New World:

> *By the introduction of this system, the negroes, far from suffering additional evils or being subjected while in a state of slavery to a more painful life than when possessed of freedom in their own country, obtain the inestimable advantage of a Knowledge of the true God and of all the benefits attendant on civilization.*

Slaveholders saw the advantages of employing Christianity to keep their bondsmen quiet and submissive. Slaves were provided ministers whose sermons urged hard work in this world in return for ease in the next world. Reverend Thomas Bacon's popular book of sermons for slaves informed them that white overseers and masters were "God's overseers." Slaves, they were told, "do all service for them, as if you did it for GOD himself."

Forced into Christianity, slaves often employed its words to fill their own needs and meanings. Its concern for the weak gave them strength. They sang songs about Jesus and heaven that carried a double meaning. Was it Jesus or liberty they sang about?

> *Run to Jesus, shun the danger,*
> *I don't expect to stay much longer here.*

When they sang about "that promised land where all is peace" was it heaven or the free territories? What did they mean when they sang:

> *Oh, freedom! oh, freedom!*
> *Oh, freedom over me!*
> *And before I'd be a slave,*
> *I'll be buried in my grave,*
> *And go home to my Lord*
> *and be free.*

But blacks continued to use Christianity as a mask for their opposition to bondage. Many black leaders in the slave South or in the North were ministers.

WHITE OPPOSITION
TO BLACK BONDAGE

A minority of whites — even though small and ineffective — always opposed oppression of red or black people. Their heroic role deserves a place in history.

In 1688 the Germantown, Pennsylvania, Quakers issued the first group protest against slavery. "To bring men hither, or to rob and sell them against their will, we stand against." They saw no reason why "these poor Negroes [have] not as much right to fight for their freedom, as you have to keep them slaves. . . ." In 1786 George Washington complained about a Philadelphia Society of Quakers that "have attempted to liberate" slaves.

Dutch colonists in New Amsterdam (New York) often violated laws to aid runaway slaves. They also permitted blacks to serve in the militia and own property, a privilege they did not grant to Jews.

Thomas Jefferson, George Washington, and Patrick Henry advocated ending slavery but took no determined action in that direction. Patrick Henry provided this explanation:

Every thinking honest man rejects slavery in Speculation, how few in practice? Would anyone believe that I am Master of slaves of my own purchase? I am drawn along by the general inconvenience of living without them; I will not, I cannot justify it.

More European Settlers Arrive

During the colonial period a veritable Tower of Babel walked down the gangplanks of European ships and spread to the far reaches of the continent. There were Belgians in Connecticut, Pennsylvania, and New Jersey; Slavs in New Mexico, Georgia, and California; Portuguese in South Carolina; Poles in Virginia and New York; Swiss in South Carolina and Pennsylvania; Russians in Alaska; Swedes, Danes, Norwegians, and Finns in Delaware, Maryland, Pennsylvania, New York, and New Jersey; Italians in Georgia, Florida, New York, Pennsylvania, Delaware, and California; French in New York, Canada, and South Carolina; Germans in Pennsylvania and New York; Greeks, Minorcans, and Corsicans in Florida; and a host of Irish Catholics and Irish Protestants, English, Scots, and Africans scattered from the eastern seaboard to the Pacific, and penetrating most of the continent.

The newcomers brought many gifts. The Scotch-Irish were known for their frontier skills, the French for their fur-trapping abilities. Among the hearty band of explorers to the interior were Italians, blacks, French, Danes, and a host of other daring men. The earliest settlers, male and female, built homes in the wilderness and made soil yield great crops. The axman's labor brought forests down and turned them into homes and furniture. Women played a vital role in frontier communities, working, cooking, and training the children in the ways of the new land.

Governor Oglethorpe of Georgia visits
a settlement of people from Scotland.

"My Dear Sweden" Melts
along the Delaware

I found in this country scarcely one genuine Swede left, the most of them are either in part or in whole on one side or other descended from English or Dutch parents, some of them have had a Dutch, German or English father, others a Swedish mother, and others a Dutch or English mother and a Swedish father. Many of them can just recollect that their grand-fathers or mothers were Swedish.

. . . The English are evidently swallowing up the people and the Swedish language is so corrupted, that if I did not know the English, it would be impossible to understand the language of my dear Sweden. Reverend Abraham Reincke, 1745

Frontiersmen from Italy

Enrico Tonti was as powerful with one hand as many others with two. During the Sicilian wars a grenade blew off his right hand, so he replaced it with one of iron. In battles with native Americans he swung it with such deadly accuracy that his foes called him "Thunder Arm." But he could do much more than fight.

In 1679 he built the *Griffin*, the first large ship to sail the Great Lakes. As second in command to French explorer Robert La Salle, he helped build Illinois' first settlement for Europeans. Three years later he and La Salle claimed the Louisiana Territory for France, which would eventually give the United States thirteen new states. In 1686 he founded Arkansas Post, a trading station that was the first European settlement in Arkansas.

Enrico's brother Alfonso led a group of explorers that settled in what became the city of Detroit. For a dozen years Alfonso Tonti was its governor, and his daughter Theresa was the first white person born in this remote outpost.

JACOB LEISLER,
IMMIGRANT AND REFORMER

Born in Frankfurt, Germany, in 1640, Jacob Leisler came to America as a young man of twenty. In 1689 he joined with others who opposed the undemocratic rule imposed on New York by wealthy Englishmen. Leisler's militia drove out the governor and his troops, and for the next few years he ruled the colony. With the aid of mechanics, storekeepers, skilled craftsmen, and small businessmen — who had been excluded from the previous government — Leisler instituted reforms.

Despite Leisler's sworn loyalty to the crown, King William in England found the steps toward self-government too dangerous to tolerate. He ordered royal troops to topple the reformers from power. In 1691 Colonel Henry Sloughter, the king's appointee as governor, arrived and placed Leisler under arrest.

His opponents demanded Leisler's execution, and before the king could hear an appeal, he was put to death. However, his institution of the New York Assembly was retained. Parliament later stated Leisler had committed no crime and the New York Assembly voted money to his heirs.

Today's government of New York owes much to the pioneering labors of this German immigrant who was executed for his audacity.

Among the many immigrant groups were the Swedes. They, like the others, worked hard adjusting to their new homeland.

Two ships launched by the Swedish West India Company landed fifty colonists near Wilmington, Delaware, in 1638. To honor their youthful queen, they named their settlement Christina. As fur and tobacco were the leading products of the colony, they soon clashed with Dutch and English in the same occupations. In 1655 Peter Stuyvesant, the Dutch governor of New Amsterdam, and his armada swallowed up the Swedish settlements without firing a shot.

By then the log cottages, with their low doors and loophole win-

John Peter Zenger vs.
Governor William Cosby

John Peter Zenger, born in Germany in 1697, came to America at the age of thirteen. Trained as a printer by William Bradford, he began publication of the *New York Weekly Journal* in 1733, immediately attacking the flagrant corruption of Governor William Cosby. Cosby was willing to use legal or illegal means to gain advantages for himself or to harm his enemies. He disfranchised all Quakers and gathered huge amounts of public funds for his private use.

Popular hatred of the governor increased the sales of Zenger's paper. Cosby tried unsuccessfully to have the Assembly and the Grand Jury indict Zenger. Finally, he prevailed upon the Provincial Council to issue a warrant for Zenger's arrest, charging "seditious libels" that inflamed the citizens.

Zenger (his papers being burned at left) was jailed, with bail set higher than his total wealth, and not permitted to see anyone for a week. The next week he communicated with his wife through the cell door and she began to publish the *Weekly Journal.*

Andrew Hamilton, who was seventy-nine and the most prominent lawyer in the colonies, took up Zenger's case. He argued simply that Zenger's printed charges were true and therefore not a libel. The "cause of liberty" was at stake, he told the jury, and they agreed. Zenger was freed and the spectators cheered. A German immigrant with a penchant for the truth, even when it struck at those high in government, risked his own liberty and won a milestone in freedom of the American press.

dows, housed a diverse population with great ambitions. In addition to tobacco and furs, the colonists raised vegetables and grain. They also accepted anyone who came from Europe — army deserters, debtors, minor criminals. Johan Printz, the three-hundred-pound governor, had only one complaint: there were not enough "true Christians."

Nearly forty years after the Dutch seizure of New Sweden, one thousand people signed an appeal for Swedish pastors, and four years later the king of Sweden sent three ministers and a collection of Bibles and hymn books. But by 1730 a preacher had to offer three services — Swedish, English, and German. Swedes were becoming assimilated with the English, Welsh, and Germans about them and, in 1776, John Morton, descendant of an original settler of New Sweden, signed the Declaration of Independence.

Germans who settled in Pennsylvania had a reputation for hard work and superstition. From the moment of their arrival, they went to work with ax and shovel. Their first home was a sod house, their next a log cabin, and their last a large stone structure. But even more important to them were the huge barns that protected livestock and harvested crops.

The German Pennsylvanian kept a garden, an orchard, and a beehive, and probably was the first to cultivate asparagus and cauliflower in America. Since their families were large, they needed all the food they raised, and everyone, including the children, helped with the farming.

The Germans brought with them a mass of folklore regarding marriage, dreams, and diseases. They were known especially for their thrift and their desire to own property. This may have grown out of the fact that most had come to the New World as indentured servants who owned nothing, not even their own labor. One English colonial governor believed that the German "industry and frugality have been the principal instruments of raising [Pennsylvania] to its present flourishing condition beyond any of his Majesty's Colonys in North America."

In 1816 an English observer made these remarks about the German farmers:

> They are a persevering, industrious people, they cultivate the earth with care, their fields have an air of neatness about them rarely to be discovered in America. The most respectable of them go on, adding dollar to dollar, and pack them up securely in an Iron chest. ... [the women] share with their husbands the labours of the field, and tend about their house as menial servants.

Religious Bigotry in America

While overshadowed by racial prejudice, animosity among white groups was also part of life in the colonies. The bigotry that stalked the lives of many Europeans in their native lands did not disappear in the New World. Catholic and Protestant Irish bitterly resented each other's presence, battled on many occasions, and often aroused the ire of other neighbors who considered both groups bellicose. In Londonderry, New Hampshire, Protestant Irish resented being considered Irish: "We were surprised to hear ourselves termed Irish people, when we so frequently ventured our all for the British Crown and Liberties against the Irish Papists." Boston's Surveyor-General of Customs lumped both groups together when he complained, "These confounded Irish will eat us all up, provisions being most extravagantly dear, and scarce. . . ."

Catholics particularly suffered discrimination at the hands of the predominant Protestant Anglo-Saxons. In New York and Maryland, "Papists" were excluded by law from citizenship rights. In 1690 a Maryland law punished any priest who entered the colony with imprisonment, death if he escaped from jail. A citizen who harbored a priest would have to stand for three days in the pillory. In 1701 Catholics in New York were prohibited from voting or holding office. When Catholics gained political power in Maryland they passed a Toleration Act. However, it did not include Unitarians, Jews, Quakers, or unbelievers. For those who did not accept the Trinity as part of their religious beliefs, the Toleration Act provided severe penalties, including death.

[45]

In the Massachusetts Bay Colony Quakers were forbidden to enter and those who did so were beaten or put to death.

CHICAGO'S FIRST NONNATIVE CITIZEN

The man called the first white settler of Chicago was not white. Jean Baptiste Pointe du Sable came from the West Indies, son of an African slave woman and French seaman. Although he gained a reputation for his frontier skills, his daring, and his ability to get along with native tribes, he was very different from rugged, white frontiersmen, like Daniel Boone, whom he knew. Du Sable was Paris-educated and an admirer of European art. His log cabin was decorated with twenty paintings he had brought from the Old World.

In 1779 du Sable established a trading post on the mouth of the Chicago River. It became the first permanent European settlement on the site, and du Sable, his native wife, Catherine, and later their two children, lived there for more than a dozen years. Although he also acquired eight hundred acres of land in Peoria, he always considered Chicago his home. The du Sable settlement included a bakehouse, dairy, smokehouse, poultry house, workshop, stable, barn, mill, and large cabin.

The first Jews to reach the New World found the same hatred that had forced them to abandon Europe. In 1654 a ship from Brazil carrying twenty-three Jews arrived in New Amsterdam. The travelers hoped to find a refuge from discrimination among the Dutch, because their homeland, Holland, had been tolerant of Jews; instead, they had to wage a three-year battle with Governor Peter Stuyvesant to remain in the colony. To the Dutch West Indian Company in the homeland, Governor Stuyvesant angrily wrote, asking permission to reject "such hateful enemies and blasphemers of the name of Christ." He charged they were "very repugnant" and "used to deceitful trading with the Christians."

Tolerance won a victory when influential Jews in Holland on the Board of Directors of the Dutch East India Company insisted that the governor accept the Jews into New Amsterdam. When the British seized the colony in 1664 and renamed it New York, Jews again had

WILLIAM PENN'S TOLERANT EXPERIMENT

William Penn, a convert to the Society of Friends (as the Quakers were known), established in Pennsylvania a haven for the persecuted. First Penn honored original land claims by paying native Americans their requested purchase prices. In 1682 he conferred with an Iroquois chief called "Emperor of Canada" about his plans for settlement. Welshmen, Rhinelanders, Irish, English, and Jews lived at peace with native Americans in Pennsylvania.

But as Quakers became more accepted and wealthy, their aims changed. Profits from the fur trade led to conflict with natives. The ethics of brotherhood changed to the ethics of the counting house. Penn's grandson struck a bargain with angry residents by agreeing to honor their demand that native scalps be redeemed at top dollar. Honor in Pennsylvania had changed with the times.

to fight for equality. Denied the right to establish a synagogue, they did win the right to worship in their homes. Finally, a century later, Parliament granted citizenship to Jews in their American colonies, providing they had resided there for seven years.

Neither the laws nor threats against the Jews or Catholics ever turned into physical violence in colonial America. The Quakers, however, became victims of violence while protesting intolerance and practices based on violence. The Massachusetts Bay Colony greeted Quakers with savage repression and death.

The Puritans considered their doctrine "the infallible and whole will of God." Soon after their landing in 1630 they announced their intention to "reduce to obedience" all they encountered. Their General Court forbade entrance to the colony except with permission of the governor. Jesuits specifically were banned under pain of death. In the campaign to enforce conformity, Puritans made church attendance compulsory; private conversations were monitored to detect anti-Puritan subversion; and taverns and homes were entered by those investigating dangerous conversations.

As opponents of war and slavery, and a people who rejected violence even in self-defense, Quakers suffered persecution in the Old

Roger Williams, who was forced to flee the Massachusetts Bay Colony because of his radical ideas was one of the few European leaders to establish harmonious relations with the native peoples he encountered.

World and the New. When they decided to challenge the Puritans, bloody conflict was inevitable.

Employing an array of tactics designed to jolt the sensibilities of the calmest enemies, they arrived at the Massachusetts Bay Colony. Quakers burst into church services to denounce Puritan ministers, shattering empty bottles to illustrate the spiritual emptiness of their words. Quaker women walked without clothes in the streets to point out the nakedness of life without true religion.

Calling them an "accursed and pernicious set of Hereticks," the Puritans concluded the devil had unleashed his vanguard upon them. They acted accordingly, whipping, branding, and driving Quakers into the wilderness. Some stubborn enough to return had their tongues bored with red-hot irons, their children seized and sold as slaves to the West Indies. The Puritan governor was convinced this tide "would not be restrained but by death." One female and five male Quakers were executed. Only the intervention of the king halted a slaughter and preserved the peace.

Alliances among the Lowly

Throughout the colonial era indentured servants, slaves, and native Americans reached out to each other. Regardless of color or background, some sensed that the same force oppressed all of them. Reward notices for slave runaways sometimes listed indentured servants who fled with them. Masters often noted that their bondsmen could speak "Indian language" or French, Spanish, or some other tongue.

In 1775 John Stuart, British officer of Southern Indian Affairs, warned that "nothing can be more alarming to Carolinians than the idea of an attack from Indians and Negroes." Their mixing together, he thought, "ought to be prevented as much as possible." Four years later a British Indian Service report stated: "Negroes infused many very bad notions in their [Indian] minds." Indeed, a logical reason for ending native slavery could have been to prevent this alliance from taking hold. If native Americans and blacks had been slaves together, natives could have led blacks in great numbers back to their land, and from there launch attacks on white settlements.

In many places laws and policy tried to keep red and black men apart. A South Carolina minister in 1725 revealed how white settlers "make Indians & Negroes a checque upon each other" lest by "their Vastly Superior Numbers we should be crushed by one or the other." In the Yemassee War of 1715 Natchez warriors attacking a settlement spared the black slaves. These served in the Natchez army, but the British also put armed blacks in the field against the black and red army.

Connecticut towns set a nine o'clock curfew for black and red men. Other towns forbade either group to come out of doors during a fire. Boston forbade either from carrying a stick or cane by day or night that "could be fit for . . . fighting or anything of that nature." In 1657 black and red men attacked Hartford, Connecticut, and set many fires. In 1727 they attacked Virginia frontier settlements.

In Spanish Mexico a similar pattern developed. Viceroy Martin Enriquez warned the king of Spain about Africans joining native societies:

> . . . it appears, Our Majesty, that the time is coming when these people will have become masters of the Indians, inasmuch as they were born among them and their maidens, and are men who dare to die as well as any Spaniard in the world. But if the Indians become corrupt and join with them, I do not know who will be in a position to resist them.

In 1537 a Mexico City plot to drive out the Spanish had black and red men joining hands. When it was betrayed, twenty-four black and red men were put to death.

In the New World, black and red people mixed, married, and often allied themselves against the Europeans who oppressed both.

Pontiac's Drive for Unity

Conflict between racial and ethnic groups often escalated when European nations went to war. In the war between the French and English that ended in 1763, the defeated French abandoned the Ohio Valley to the British. For ten native societies, this was their land and they had no intention of surrendering it to the British, whom they hated. An Ottawa chief named Pontiac commanded the loyalty of eighteen tribes. In 1762 he told the British:

> *Englishmen, although you have conquered the French, you have not yet conquered us. We are not your slaves. These lakes, these woods, and mountains were left us by our ancestors. They are our inheritance; and we will part with them to none.*

Pontiac was also fearful of the European impact upon his people. Repeatedly he urged them to reject the liquor and firearms of their enemies, since it did nothing but make them weak and dependent. A return to their ancient ways was necessary for strength. He said:

> *My children, you have forgotten the customs and traditions of your forefathers. Why do you not clothe yourselves in skins, as they did, use bows and arrows and the stone-pointed lances, which they used? You have bought guns, knives, kettles and blankets from the white man until you can no longer do without them; and what is worse you have drunk the poison firewater, which turns you into fools. Fling all these things away; live as your wise forefathers did before you.*

Chief Pontiac meeting with British officers.

In 1763 the "Paxton Boys" massacred
defenseless Indians at Lancaster, Pennsylvania.

With tribal support mounting, Pontiac struck British forts in the Ohio Valley. In several weeks they overwhelmed eight, their lightning raids catching the British off guard. The man most surprised and angered by Pontiac's victories was Sir Jeffery Amherst, commander of British forces in North America. His surprise turned to rage.

General Amherst proposed what might be called the "final solution" to the problem. Writing to his assistant Colonel Henry Bouquet, Amherst recommended he "send the smallpox among" the forces of Pontiac. It could be spread "by means of blankets," he noted. Colonel Bouquet agreed to make the effort. Further, he suggested training savage dogs to track down and destroy "that vermin." Pleased with this response, General Amherst urged the colonel to continue to think creatively about "every method" to wipe out "this execrable race." "I wish to hear of no prisoners," he informed Colonel Bouquet. A smallpox epidemic was soon raging among Pontiac's men.

The genocidal approach advocated by Sir Jeffrey Amherst was put into practice within a few months. Some fifty-seven settlers from Paxton, Pennsylvania, swooped down upon a peaceful Conestoga village and killed all they found — three men, two women, and a boy. The governor speedily placed the remaining Conestogas under protective custody in the Lancaster jail.

The Paxton mob then marched on the city, broke into the prison and murdered the Conestogas. This destruction came without provocation or warning, and it ended the existence of the Conestogas, a people whom whites had always regarded as friendly.

Frontier colonists lived by the policies advocated by Sir Jeffery Amherst. Robert Rogers, commander of Rogers's Rangers, wrote a five-act play that glorified the policy of genocide toward natives. It clearly showed the economic motives of the British in wanting to rid the country of its original inhabitants. Said one character:

These hateful Indians kidnap all the game. Curse their black heads. . . . 'Twere to be wished not one of them survived, thus to infest the world and plague mankind. Cursed heathen infidels! Mere savage beasts! They don't deserve to breathe in Christian air, and should be hunted down like other brutes.

[57]

In the next scene two British hunters murder and scalp two natives. "Ready cash, two hundred crowns" is their reward for this act.

After Pontiac's successful raids the British moved to protect the frontier from further bloodshed. The Proclamation of 1763 forbade any white settlements in the Ohio Valley. The British did not want colonists where they would have difficulty protecting them. They also wanted the colonists close to the eastern seaboard where tax agents and merchants would find them easy to reach. Among those vigorously protesting the new policy were George Washington, Patrick Henry, and Benjamin Franklin. Each had investments in companies owning native land in the Ohio Valley -- Washington in the Mississippi Company, Henry in the Ohio Company, and Franklin in the Walpole Company.

"All Men Are Created Equal"

Before the ringing words of the Declaration of Independence made unity among the colonists imperative, there was profound disagreement over whether such sentiments applied even to whites. Thomas Jefferson feared too many settlers from overseas would endanger American institutions. He favored "a more homogeneous, more peaceable, more durable government." His lifelong opponent, Alexander Hamilton, agreed.

Benjamin Franklin warned about the dangers of unrestricted immigration. Pointing out that a third of Pennsylvania was of German birth, he asked, "Why should the Palatine boors be suffered to swarm into our settlements, and by herding together, establish their language and manners to the exclusion of ours?" He felt badly about the "very small . . . number of purely white people in the world."

Franklin had a very narrow definition of white people. Along with Germans, he condemned "Spaniards, Italians, French, Russians, and Swedes" as people with a "swarthy complexion." Admit the "lovely white and red" people, he urged and reject "the sons of Africa" and "all blacks and tawneys." But no steps to restrict immigration would be taken for a hundred years.

To defeat the British, Americans had to forge the strangest unity. The Revolutionary Army accepted citizens and immigrants, those who could or could not speak English, white, red, and black men, Catholic, Protestant, and Jew, foreigners from France, Haiti, Poland, and Germany. When it suddenly rejected black enlistments, it did so because southern slaveholders demanded this as the price of unity. When it accepted black volunteers again, it did so because the British had offered slaves who escaped to their lines freedom and an opportunity to fight against their former masters.

From the Boston Massacre in 1770 to the British surrender at Yorktown in 1781, minorities and foreigners contributed substantially to the long fight for an America free of English control. A leader of Boston citizens the night of the fight with the British was Crispus Attucks, a runaway slave. Two centuries after Bostonians placed his body in the martyr's grave, historians were still questioning his courage and his color. Some have insisted he was really a Natick Indian. Others have held that Attucks was too drunk to know what he was doing.

The only Catholic to sign the Declaration of Independence was Charles Carroll, an Irishman and the wealthiest of the signers. Thousands of other poor Irish served in the patriot army and navy. So did five thousand black men. At Bunker Hill Peter Salem shot the British commander. But after the war some blacks who had been promised their freedom for helping to liberate America were returned to slavery. Those who fled to the British found themselves sold into slavery in the West Indies.

"Swamp Fox" Marion, a Scotch-Irish American, led white and black men against British forces in the Carolinas in a series of daring guerrilla raids. At Valley Forge, German General Von Steuben restored discipline to a deteriorating army. Francis Salvador, a South

Above left: Peter Muhlenberg, a German minister, urged his congregation to support the cause of American Independence.

Above right: Baron von Steuben brought discipline and training to George Washington's ragged army, even at Valley Forge.

Below: At the Battle of Bunker Hill Peter Salem brought down the British Major Pitcairn.

Carolina Jew, rode twenty-eight miles on horseback to warn his countrymen that the British were coming. Guiseppe Vigo, an Italian, guided the patriot army 250 miles to capture Fort Vincennes, and avoided execution as a spy by swallowing a document before the British could question him. Count Casimir Pulaski of Poland, who volunteered his services to Washington, was killed at the battle of Savannah in 1779 leading a cavalry charge.

ST. PATRICK'S DAY
AT VALLEY FORGE

George Washington's bedraggled army included so many Irishmen that they demanded the right to celebrate St. Patrick's Day at Valley Forge in 1780. The general was dubious, but the Irish were persistent. After he agreed, General Washington warned his Irish soldiers to be sure "that the celebration of the Day will not be attended with the least Rioting or Disorder." He also had heard about the Irish reputation for fighting.

Top left: During the American Revolution Count Casimir Pulaski of Poland was shot while commanding a cavalry regiment raid near Savannah, Georgia.

Top right: Thaddeus Kosciusko helped fight for American Independence and later urged liberation of slaves.

Bottom left: Deborah Sampson disguised herself as a man and served with the Massachusetts regiment during the American Revolution.

Bottom right: Margaret Cochran Corbin was badly wounded in the American Revolution when she took her dead husband's place during the Battle of Fort Washington.

A New Nation

At the time the great words of the Declaration of Independence were written, every fifth person in America was a slave. Not only did the historic document fail to liberate bondsmen, but it also failed to mention bondage at all. A section of the original document blaming King George III for imposing both the slave trade and slavery on the colonies was dropped from the final version. It had categorically denounced slavery as a "cruel war against human nature itself, violating its most sacred right of life and liberty in the persons of a distant people." It was vetoed by two southern delegations to the Continental Congress.

As the colonists moved toward emancipation from British tyranny, black Americans asked for liberty. A black petition to the Massachusetts General Court in 1773 asked for freedom: "We have no property! we have no wives! we have no children! no city! no country!"

The next year, another Massachusetts resident, Abigail Adams, wrote to her husband, John. "It always appeared a most iniquitous scheme to me to fight ourselves for what we are daily robbing and plundering from those who have as good a right to freedom as we have." John Adams would sit on the committee of three in the Continental Congress that drafted the Declaration of Independence and its statement that "all men are created equal." No man was prepared to grant women the equality they promised themselves.

The new government and its new Constitution provided slaveholders with protection for their property. In three separate sections

LUCY TERRY AND
THE PRINCE FAMILY

Few women in America would rise to the heights in colonial times achieved by Lucy Terry, a slave. Kidnapped in Africa at age five, she was brought to Deerfield, Massachusetts, in 1735. On the frontier between British and French colonies, the tiny hamlet was often under siege from native tribes allied with the foreigners. In 1746, when Lucy Terry was sixteen, she wrote a poem about a raid. Considered the best depiction of the event recorded, it also became the first poem written in the New World by an African.

Lucy gained her freedom when she married Abijah Prince. a black man who had been granted his liberty. Abijah purchased Lucy's freedom and the two established a home on tracts of land given to him. Two of the Princes' sons saw service in the American Revolution.

After the war Lucy Terry Prince waged a long battle against white hatred. When a neighbor tore down her fences and set her haystacks ablaze, she carried her protest to the Vermont Governor's Council, and won her point. When her youngest son, Abijah, Jr., applied to Williams College, she addressed the trustees for three hours on their obligation to accept black and white students. But she was informed the prohibition against blacks stood.

Once more she appeared in court, this time fighting a boundary-line dispute with a neighbor in Sunderland, Vermont. She not only won the case, but also was credited by the judge with a better argument than he "had heard from any lawyer at the Vermont bar."

of the Constitution, property in slaves was given federal protection. One provided federal aid in recapturing slaves who fled across state boundaries. Another gave the infamous African slave trade twenty more years to wind up its business. Another section awarded slave-holding regions extra voting power in Congress, each African to be counted as three-fifths of a man. In none of the sections on slavery was the word used. The great charter of the first Republican government in the world would not include the word "slave." This deception remained.

The new Constitution did deal with religious differences among white men. It forbade religious tests for men who would be elected to office in the new nation. No longer could a Catholic, Jew, or Quaker be denied office because he was not considered of the correct religion. The Bill of Rights extended religious freedom even further. Congress was forbidden from giving any church special preference or passing any laws that would affect religion in America. All churches had a right to exist, and members of any creed could serve in the government.

The Founding Fathers, however, failed to mention the legal rights of women. It was a male-dominated society that gave all rights to men — including the rights of women. Adult women basically were considered as children, under the charge of a husband or father, with no real rights save those he wished to grant.

As for the blacks, one of the most advanced thinkers in the new nation, Thomas Jefferson, believed that Africans "require less sleep," "are more ardent after their female," "their griefs are transient," and "their existence appears to participate more of sensation than reflection." Compared to Europeans, Jefferson found Africans "much inferior" in reasoning, "in imagination they are dull, tasteless." Even Dr. Benjamin Rush, a leading antislavery voice of the era, thought that the African's skin color stemmed from endemic leprosy. The views expressed by Jefferson and Rush strengthened the arguments of those who sought to perpetuate slavery.

But the depth of racist thinking at this early date, even among the enlightened, is best illustrated by a paper presented by Benjamin Franklin on free blacks. While his 1789 paper failed to find any innate inferiority among blacks, nevertheless Franklin found that conditions had reduced the black to less than a man:

> *The unhappy man, who has long been treated as a brute animal, too frequently sinks beneath the common standard of the human species.*

*Gustavas Vasa captured in Benin, Africa, at the
age of eleven and brought as a slave
to America, was one of many blacks who took a
leading part in denouncing slavery and the slave trade.*

The galling chains that bind his body do also fetter his intellectual faculties, and impair the social affections of his heart. Accustomed to move like a mere machine, by the will of the master, reflection is suspended; he has not the power of choice; and reason and conscience have but little influence over his conduct, because he is chiefly governed by the passion of fear. . . . Under such circumstances freedom may often prove a misfortune to himself and prejudicial to society.

When all racist arguments for inequality had been put to rest, this one, utilizing sociological jargon, would be summoned forth to justify injustice from that day to this.

Many of the Founding Fathers thought that the Constitution had placed slavery on the road to extinction. Many delegates abhorred it and there was talk of its early demise. The Northwest Ordinance of 1787 forbade slavery north and west of the Ohio River, while in the northeastern states it was doomed by the movement toward abolition. By permitting Congress to ban the slave trade in twenty years, the delegates had prepared a means of halting slavery at its African source. Perhaps many delegates left Philadelphia believing the compromise they had made with slaveowners was unimportant since slavery was slowly dying.

Events proved otherwise. The invention of the cotton gin six years later made slavery more lucrative than ever. More Africans were imported and more land purchased for slavery and cotton. Masters and bondsmen swarmed across the continent, and plantations grew in Mississippi, Alabama, Arkansas, and Missouri. Now, no Northwest Ordinance kept slaveholders from trying to plant their institution in the free soil of the old Northwest. Now, no congressional ban against the slave trade kept greedy merchants and captains from importing Africans. More were brought to the plantations of the New World than when the trade was legal. The invention of the cotton gin and the passage of the first Federal Fugitive Slave Law occurred in 1793. There was a connection between the two events that was not accidental.

The "Reign
of the
Witches"

Less than a hundred days after George Washington was inaugurated as first president of the United States, a revolution erupted in France. Americans greeted the news enthusiastically. The overthrow of despotism in France, however, would eventually divide the American people and lead to the first repression of ethnic minorities in the new nation.

Among the original French enthusiasts were recent arrivals to America — largely Irish, French, and German immigrants. They organized themselves into Democratic-Republican societies and rallied around the new political alliance being shaped by Thomas Jefferson. By 1898 fifty pro-Jefferson clubs were formed, the first being the German Republican Society, which began in Philadelphia in 1793.

Soon Jefferson's Federalist opponents charged that the French Revolution was stimulating subversion by foreigners in America. Jefferson, they claimed, was the leader. "It has long been suspected that secret societies, under the influence and direction of France, holding principles subversive of our religion and government, exist somewhere in this country," Reverend Jedediah Morse warned ominously. "We have in truth secret enemies whose professed design is to subvert and overturn our holy religion."

Federalist papers played on the popular fear that recent immigrants constituted a foreign conspiracy — and attributed this to supporters of Thomas Jefferson. Joseph Hopkinson, author of the patriotic song "Hail, Columbia," sounded a fearful note: "The time approaches when the American knee shall bend before the footstool of foreigners, and the dearest rights and interests of our country await on their nod." There was talk by Fisher Ames that "Kentucky is all alien," by which he meant "men who are averse to the wholesome restrictions of society." Other Federalists warned of "vile incendiary publications of foreign hirelings among us."

ALBERT GALLATIN, SWISS IMMIGRANT

Albert Gallatin, born in Geneva, Switzerland, arrived in America while still in his teens. Settling in Pennsylvania, he was elected to the state constitutional convention and later to the legislature. But when he was elected to the United States Senate in 1793, his troubles began. When he publicly asked Alexander Hamilton to show how government finances had been handled since the beginning of the government, Gallatin became a target of Federalist anger. Although Gallatin had lived in America for thirteen years, they charged he was not properly naturalized as a citizen. Senators warned about the danger of foreigners, and his Senate seat was taken away.

When Hamilton and George Washington led an army to suppress the "Whiskey Rebellion," Gallatin hastily warned the farmers to avoid a bloody confrontation. Again Hamilton was furious, since he sought the incident to instill fear of the new government in the hearts of the poor and oppressed. Gallatin's efforts frustrated Hamilton's.

After six years as a Jeffersonian congressman, Gallatin was appointed the Secretary of the Treasury in Jefferson's cabinet. His brilliance and diligence brought order out of federal finances. During the War of 1812 he tried to bring peace, traveling to Russia to seek mediation of the conflict. Later he helped negotiate the Treaty of Ghent that concluded the war.

Gallatin was a friend to and an expert on native societies, and helped promote their study by the American Ethnological Society, which he founded. His greatest contribution was his knowledge of finance and banking, freely contributed to the country of his adoption.

The antiforeign rhetoric soon turned to demands for legislation against subversion, aimed at Jefferson's Irish and French supporters. The Albany *Sentinel* urged, "When the state is in danger and strong remedies are necessary . . . none but an enemy can resist their use." Within a three-week period in 1798, Congress passed three laws against aliens. One changed the residence requirement for prospective citizens from five to fourteen years. The others permitted the president to deport without trial any alien he considered "dangerous to the peace and safety" of the country, or any alien during wartime. A week later Congress passed the Sedition Act, which could be directed against aliens and citizens who displeased the party in power — the Federalists. Any writing or oral statement against the government or any of its officers became a criminal act. Heavy fines and imprisonment awaited those found guilty under it.

Although these laws were not uniformly enforced, and their aim was to destroy the political party led by Jefferson, they struck terror in the hearts of both aliens and friends of Jefferson and of the French Revolution. America's first political witch hunt, with Irish, German, and French minorities as the prime targets, was underway.

The most famous victim of the repression was Matthew Lyon, an Irish-born indentured servant who had once been sold to a farmer for two horses. A Jeffersonian congressman who fearlessly expressed his belief in democratic principles, Lyon was called "ragged Mat, the Democrat" by his enemies. He was arrested for making fun of President John Adams in a private letter and given four months in jail, with a thousand-dollar fine. In prison he was reelected to Congress.

President John Adams and Secretary of State Thomas Pickering made immediate appeals for strict enforcement of the new laws. Pickering announced that he found "the United Irishmen" the most dangerous of "Alien Scoundrels." President Adams accelerated the hysteria by denouncing "the influx of foreigners and discontented characters" who might turn the land toward "malevolence and turbulence, for the outcasts of the universe." Later President Adams would insist that his hands had remained clean, that he had never ordered any prosecutions under the new laws.

Many aliens were arrested, many editors friendly to the cause of France intimidated, and many more recent arrivals from Europe became so panicky that they fled the country. A group of scholars who wished to return to France to escape American repression was refused passports by President Adams. His remarks indicate the anti-intellectualism of the movement against Jefferson and the aliens:

We have had too many French philosophers already and I really begin to think, or rather to suspect, that learned academics, not under the immediate inspection and control of the government, have disorganized the world, and are incompatible with the social order.

For all the fear they spread, the Alien and Sedition acts boomeranged. Not foreigners nor Jeffersonians but Federalists were the final victims. The laws united the supporters of Jefferson, drove citizens to their cause, and soiled the reputation of the Federalists, whose new laws were a threat to constitutional government. Ethnic groups within the nation rallied to Jefferson's Democratic-Republicans, and in 1800 helped elect him president of the United States. The "reign of the witches," as the new president called it, had ended.

URIAH P. LEVY,
NAVAL HERO AND REFORMER

In 1802 a ten-year-old boy fled his home in Philadelphia to begin a career on the open seas. Uriah P. Levy at twenty was captain of a ship he partly owned and soon a hero of the War of 1812. In 1817 he began a long, turbulent, and honorable career in the United States Navy. Shunned because he was Jewish, Captain Levy was court-martialed six times for minor infractions of the law. Battling against his treatment every time, he won vindication and his old rank.

He carried on a long campaign to eliminate the flogging of sailors. His campaign received official recognition by the navy in 1862, the year Commodore Uriah P. Levy died.

Black Laws
and Black
Resistance

In the years following the American Revolution, the northern states gave up slavery and the southern states fastened it down securely. Southern blacks, slave and free, could not own property or bear arms, vote or testify in court, or raise an arm in defense of their families. Whites could sell, auction, will or raffle blacks, or win or lose them at cards. They could punish, maim, and even execute them as they chose.

From the beginning slave resistance to white control took many forms. Slaves resorted to poison, arson, and sabotage to rid themselves of evil masters and overseers. Slave plots and rebellions marked the colonial era. "The love of freedom, sir, is an inborn sentiment," warned a Carolina planter. "It springs forth and flourishes with a vigor that defies all check. There never have been slaves in any country who have not seized the first favorable opportunity to revolt."

Slave plots involving men and women were discovered from colonial New York to Georgia. In 1712 slave insurrections struck New York, leaving nine whites dead. In 1740 a major revolt rocked Stono, South Carolina, and the next year another exploded in New York. In the first an eyewitness reported:

. . . A number of Negroes having assembled together at Stono, first surprised and killed two young men in a ware-house, and then plundered it of guns and ammunition. Being thus provided with arms, they elected one of their number captain, and agreed to follow him, marching towards the south-west, with colours flying and drums beating, like a disciplined company . . . .

[73]

Slave resistance marked the entire era of bondage in the Americas. Black men and women fled their masters, planned revolts or sabotaged their work. In this old print armed whites pursue blacks into swamps where they had fled.

In 1800, as the Jeffersonians came to political power, a massive slave rebellion was uncovered in Henrico County, Virginia. Gabriel Prosser and his followers planned to capture Richmond, sparing no one except the French and Quakers. The first, he reasoned, were enemies of the Americans and the second were known enemies of bondage.

Gabriel's band was defeated, not by superior forces but by a driving rainstorm. The night his men planned to march on Richmond, rains washed out bridges and roads. Before they could regroup, the plan was betrayed and its leaders arrested.

Governor James Monroe, a leading Jeffersonian and a future president, ordered six hundred militia to smash the conspiracy. He personally questioned the prisoners. One told the statesman:

I have nothing more to offer than what General Washington would have had to offer, had he been taken by the British officers and put to trial by them. I have ventured my life in endeavoring to obtain the liberty of my countrymen, and am a willing sacrifice in their cause.

Governor Monroe agreed that the rebels must be put to death. The insurrection, he felt, "embraced most of the slaves in this city and neighborhood [and] pervaded other parts, if not the whole, of the state."

Neither Monroe nor other Jeffersonians saw the importance of including blacks in their definition of those requiring freedom. Neither did they reason that the blood bath they had averted with Prosser's men might be permanently postponed if they abandoned slavery.

Not all resistance took so violent a form. Learning to read or write violated the slave codes, but slaves secretly did. In times of stress, when, for example, slaves feared they or their children would be sold, they fled to the woods until the crisis passed. Through songs and religious music, slaves expressed their longing for liberty and their love for each other. The black community on each plantation tried as best it could to protect its members, to provide for its ill or weak, and to convince masters and overseers to respect its humanity.

[75]

SLAVE REVOLT IN HAITI

In August, 1791, a half million Africans rose against their French masters in Haiti. Led by Toussaint L'Ouverture, a fifty-year-old slave coachman, they battled for ten years against Spanish, French, and English soldiers, and drove them into the sea. A white historian reported: "The Negroes are spirited and brave, patient in adversity, meeting death and torture with the most undaunted fortitude. Their conduct in the most trying situations approaching even to heroism; no Negro sighs, groans, or complains."

By 1803 the island was free. The revolutionists declared, "Restored to our primitive dignity, we have asserted our rights; we swear never to yield them to any power on earth." This was the only completely successful slave revolt in human history.

The revolt had an important effect on America. Napoleon had learned how hard it was to protect this French possession so far from the homeland. He wondered whether he could really protect the Louisiana Territory. When President Thomas Jefferson sent ambassadors to buy New Orleans, Napoleon offered the entire Louisiana land. America suddenly doubled its land size — at four cents an acre!

Historian John Hope Franklin has noted: "It was the Negroes of Haiti that were, to a large degree, responsible for the acquisition of Louisiana by the United States and, it might be added, the westward movement."

Free blacks in the South lived a precarious existence. Slaveholders were fearful that their very presence undermined bondage. Legislatures in the new nation increasingly restricted their rights and some demanded they leave the state. Denied power, the black community nevertheless organized its resources to deal with such crises. Mutual aid societies for blacks were organized in both the North and South, providing sickness and death benefits. In Virginia blacks owned sixty thousand dollars in church property, managed their affairs in

Petersburgh and Norfolk, kept all records, and paid (but were not always allowed to select) the white minister.

The position of free northern black men and women was hardly less precarious. Some states prohibited their migration and others demanded the posting of bonds too expensive for poor people. Separate schools, churches, and neighborhoods created black ghettos long before the Civil War. Nevertheless, blacks united to help each other, to build their own schools and churches, and to make community life bearable and warm despite white hostility.

Even the western territories and states discriminated against black men and women. In 1803 Indiana passed a law prohibiting black testimony in court. Four years later it forbade blacks to serve in the militia or to vote. A three-dollar yearly poll tax was also required of each black in the state. If the West provided a free and new experience for whites, it generally presented the same old brick wall of resistance for blacks.

Neither the wealthy nor educated black escaped northern animosity. In 1811 a black teen-ager at the graduation exercises of his segregated New York high school asked his classmates some pointed questions:

> *What are my prospects? To what shall I turn my hand? Shall I be a mechanic? No one will employ me; white boys won't work with me. Shall I be a merchant? No one will have me in his office. Can you be surprised at my discouragement?*

Although the reign of terror initiated for foreign whites by the Alien and Sedition Act passed after a few years, it never vanished for free blacks. The kidnapping of free blacks for sale in the South as slaves was frequent. The Quakers of Philadelphia repeatedly came to the aid of blacks seized by slave-catchers and often carried petitions against this evil to the Congress. Bishop Richard Allen, founder of the African Methodist Episcopal (A.M.E.) church in America, was one of those seized in Philadelphia. Unlike most hapless blacks caught in this web, he was able to summon so many white witnesses that the kidnapper was himself jailed.

[77]

Led by such outstanding figures as Bishop Richard Allen, Reverend Absolom Jones, and James Forten, a wealthy sailmaker, black intellectuals contemplated a massive move to Africa to escape discrimination in the free North. Their African Institution, with branches in large cities, was actively planning a return to the ancestral homeland, and Paul Cuffe, a wealthy New Bedford sea captain, actually took thirty-eight black Americans to Africa at his own expense. But if some blacks were already seeking to escape from the land of the free, its promise was hardly being fulfilled.

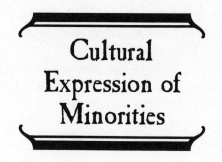

Cultural Expression of Minorities

Red and black men and women tried to learn the ways of whites without losing their own identity. This was a difficult task, since whites usually insisted that other cultures were wrong and needed to conform to their ideas. Besides, in promoting Christianity among nonwhites, Europeans sought to weaken the hold of their original culture. A people without a strong faith in themselves, their history, and culture is easy to defeat and control.

But the whites offered important tools and methods worth using. The native tribes made excellent use of the horses from Europe, better use in warfare than did the settlers. Blacks used church and work songs to communicate their love of freedom, their belief in a better day. Mexican-Americans accepted the Christianity of the Spaniards and in turn infused European ways with their own unique contributions. Their skills with horses, lariats, and firearms enriched the history and folklore of the Southwest.

In the years following the War of 1812, the Cherokees wondered how to live with the settlers. They agreed that they must not sell or give any more land to the newcomers. To prevent whites from purchasing land from any Cherokee they could find and convince through liquor or persuasion, they made death the penalty for any Cherokee who sold the nation's land.

On the other hand, Cherokees felt whites had an important discovery in the use of a written language that could be put on paper and read. Most native tribes communicated entirely through talking and had no written language other than pictures. History was conveyed from generation to generation by the village elders. The Cherokees did not, however, want to learn and adopt the English language. That would destroy their own civilization.

After working several years, Sequoyah, a Cherokee scholar, invented a language for his nation. His alphabet of eighty-five characters put into written form the tongue Cherokees had used for hundreds of years. Children and adults were quickly able to learn the new written form and soon illiteracy in the tribe disappeared. Several years later the Cherokees met to write their own constitution, one that promised its citizens peace and "our common welfare." By the next year Cherokees started a newspaper with their own printing press. White as well as red people read the *Cherokee Phoenix*, since it was published in both Cherokee and English.

Americans from Africa were also contributing to the culture of the new nation. Phillis Wheatley, a New England slave and poet, became the second woman in America to have a volume of poems published. When she sent General George Washington a poem praising his fight for American Independence, he asked her to visit him at Cambridge. The poet and the slaveholder met, but there is no record of their conversation.

In the field of science, Benjamin Banneker, a free black from Maryland, made several contributions. He constructed a clock, the first in America. For ten years he published almanacs that told of the tides, crops, moon, and sun. At Thomas Jefferson's suggestion, he was appointed to the committee of surveyors that planned the city of Washington, D.C. In his almanacs and in his correspondence with Jefferson, he repeatedly urged an end to slavery and discrimination.

His efforts had little effect, however. In 1806 when Banneker died, Jefferson sat in the White House, but Banneker could no longer vote in Maryland. Three years before, his state repealed a law that had allowed free black men to vote.

David Rittenhouse, Scientist

No one in America knew better than the Rittenhouse family how much the new country was a land of liberty and opportunity. In the seventeenth century one Dutch-German Rittenhouse became America's first papermaker and then the first Mennonite bishop. He was the great-grandfather of David Rittenhouse, who also was known for his inventions. David's mother, Elizabeth, had been orphaned as a child and grown up a Quaker in an age that viewed them as strange if not dangerous.

A thin and sickly lad, young David began reading the scientific works of Isaac Newton and Benjamin Franklin when he was eleven, and soon built himself a workshop. When an Irish schoolteacher, Thomas Barton, arrived in town, life changed at the Rittenhouse home. Barton fell in love with Esther, David's sister. He taught David Greek, Latin, French, and philosophy. David became a clock-maker; he developed a telescope and surveying instruments, including America's first compass.

He went on to greater fame as surveyor of the famous Mason-Dixon line, and then as president of the American Philosophical Society. In 1769 and with his own telescope he estimated the sun was 92,940,000 miles from earth. Today scientists reckon it as 92,900,000.

When George Washington read his farewell speech to his troops on Christmas Eve 1783 he peered through a pair of glasses made by David Rittenhouse.

A sickly young farmboy born to German immigrant and Quaker parents had gone far in the new land.

Tecumtha
and the War
of 1812

For the most part, whites ignored the cultures of nonwhites. Their major interest in these peoples was in confiscating their land and benefiting from their labors.

Long before his bloodthirsty reputation as an Indian fighter swept him into the White House, William Henry Harrison sought to seize native lands through fraud and deception. Relying on rum, threats of violence, and other means as his diplomatic approach, General Harrison won the titles of lands in Illinois, Indiana, Ohio, Michigan, and Wisconsin. Negotiated in fifteen treaties by various tribal spokesmen selected by the general, they were usually enacted under duress or drunkenness.

General Harrison's approach worked well until it was challenged by Tecumtha, a Shawnee spokesman. Calling on his people to reject the white man's ways, his alcohol, and his treaties, Tecumtha urged all natives to unite regardless of tribe. His philosophical position was that whites are "never contented, but always encroaching" on the natives and their land. He urged "all the red men to unite in claiming a common and equal right in the land, as it was at first, and should be yet; for it was never divided, but belongs to all, for the use of each." The crux of his argument held that no person could sell the land to each other or strangers, unless all agree: "Any sale not made by all is not valid."

During the War of 1812 Tecumtha joined forces with the British and managed to capture Detroit. Some three thousand Indians of many tribes took up arms under Tecumtha. But when the British appointed Colonel Henry Proctor, a spineless and frightened man, to command their forces, there was no chance of defeating the United States. Before he died in 1813, Tecumtha confronted Proctor, who had advised the natives under his command to massacre prisoners, and said, "I conquer to save, and you to murder." But Tecumtha's unifying concepts died with him.

Unlike most native Americans who sided with the British, blacks played an important part in land and sea victories for the United States during the war of 1812. Every sixth man in the navy was black. Commodore Perry objected to a group of black seamen sent to him by a Commodore Chauncey. "I have yet to learn that the color of a man's skin or the cut and trimming of the coat can effect a man's qualifications or usefulness," responded Chauncey. After the Battle of Lake Erie, Perry admitted his black sailors had been among the bravest.

As the British forces approached New Orleans in 1812, Andrew Jackson appealed to the city's black population to come to its defense. A proud group of blacks volunteered and lined up with Choctaw tribesmen and irregular troops to head off the British invasion. A fog descended as the British landed and the sharp two-hour battle resulted in a total American victory. General Edward Pakenham lay among the 1,500 British dead, picked off by a famous black marksman.

When an army paymaster decided to withhold pay for Jackson's red and black troops, Jackson ordered him to reward all "without inquiring whether the troops are white, black or tea." A huge New Orleans crowd welcomed their returning heroes of all colors.

Florida's Red and Black Freedom-Fighters

Perhaps nowhere on the continent was American opposition to peaceful life by nonwhites more unrelenting or destructive than in Florida. Slaves from the English colonies (and then the southern states) fled to this lush, Spanish colony and settled among the Seminole societies. Some formed their own colonies, and carried on trade and peaceful relations with neighboring tribes of black and red people. For fifty miles along the Appalachicola River, field and farmlands owned by black and red men and women prospered. Families peacefully grew to maturity, and children played in the clearings.

The only interruption of this scene came from repeated invasions by southern slave-catchers, seeking to reclaim their human property. There was mounting anger among slaveholders in America, who saw this successful colony in Florida as a beckoning light for their discontented slaves and as proof that blacks could turn freedom into economic success.

By 1816 General Andrew Jackson ordered an invasion of Florida to "return the stolen Negroes and property to their rightful owners." Creek mercenaries, regular soldiers, and naval vessels converged on Fort Negro, built by the British during the War of 1812 and left to black and red warriors under Garcia, a black leader. To American demands of surrender, Garcia laughed in the face of a delegation and hoisted the Union Jack and a red flag. The battle commenced.

A heated cannonball from a navy ship hit the ammunition dump and tore the fort to pieces. Most of the three hundred people inside were killed, and the rest were led back to slavery in Georgia. But until the 1840s black and red resistance continued. The Third Seminole War, as it was called, proved to be America's most costly engagement with natives in history and failed to break the nonwhite resistance. Families lived and fought on.

"THERE ARE GOOD WHITE MEN . . ."

(About half a century before the Third Seminole War, in 1787 when the new Constitution was written, it offered native Americans no rights or recognition. Previous treaties protecting property or families were nullified. That year a Delaware chief, Pachgantachilias, gave his opinion about the citizens of the new nation:)

I admit that there are good white men, but they bear no proportion to the bad, the bad must be the strongest for they rule. They do what they please. They enslave those who are not of their own color. . . . They would make slaves of us if they could; but as they cannot do it, they kill us. There is no faith to be placed in their words.

Bibliography

The Council on Interracial Books for Children. *Chronicles of American Indian Protest*. Greenwich, Conn.: Fawcett Publications, 1971.

Cavanah, Frances, ed. *We Came to America*. Philadelphia: Macrae Smith Company, 1954.

Franklin, John Hope. *From Slavery to Freedom*. New York: Alfred A. Knopf, 1967.

Handlin, Oscar. *The Uprooted*. New York: Grosset & Dunlap, 1951.

Handlin, Oscar, ed. *Immigration as a Factor in American History*. Englewood Cliffs, N.J.: Prentice-Hall, Inc., 1959.

Higham, John. *Strangers in the Land*. New York: Atheneum, 1971.

Hoff, Rhoda, ed. *America's Immigrants*. New York: Henry Z. Walck, Inc., 1967.

Hofstadter, Richard, and Wallace, Michael, eds. *American Violence*. New York: Random House, 1970.

Josephy, Alvin M., Jr. *The Indian Heritage of America*. New York: Alfred A. Knopf, 1968.

Katz, William Loren. *Eyewitness: The Negro in American History*. New York: Pitman and Company, 1967.

Kennedy, John F. *A Nation of Immigrants*. New York: Popular Library, 1964.

McWilliams, Carey. *North from Mexico*. New York: Greenwood Press, 1968.

Rose, Peter I., ed. *Many Peoples, One Nation*. New York: Random House, 1973.

Schappes, Morris U., ed. *A Documentary History of the Jews in the United States 1654–1875*. New York: The Citadel Press, 1952.

Senior, Clarence. *Our Citizens from the Caribbean*. New York: McGraw-Hill, 1965.

Shannon, William V. *The American Irish*. New York: The Macmillan Company, 1963.

Wittke, Carl. *We Who Built America*. Western Reserve, Ohio: Western Reserve University, 1964.

Wright, Kathleen. *The Other Americans: Minorities in American History*. Los Angeles: Lawrence Publishing Co., 1969.

Index